Jim Morrison

James Douglas Morrison (December 8, 1943 – July 3, 1971) was an American singer, songwriter and poet, who served as the lead vocalist of the rock band the Doors. Due to his poetic lyrics, distinctive voice, wild personality, unpredictable and erratic performances, and the dramatic circumstances surrounding his life and early death, Jim Morrison is regarded by music critics and fans as one of the most iconic and influential frontmen in rock history. Since his death, his fame has endured as one of popular culture's most rebellious and oft-displayed icons, representing the generation gap and youth counterculture.

JIM MORRISON

Quotes and Poems

QUOTES AND POEMS
by JIM MORRISON

Published by

Delhi Open Books

G/F, 4771/23, Bharat Ram Road, Daryaganj, New Delhi-110002
Ph.: 91-11-42408081
E-mail: delhiopenbooks2016@gmail.com

ISBN: 9789389847321

Cover, Typesetting, and Book Design by **ROHIT**

Contents

THE DOORS

Moment of inner freedom
when the mind is opened & the
infinite universe revealed
& the soul is left to wander
dazed & confus'd searching
here & there for teachers & friends.

People need Connectors
Writers, heroes, stars, leaders
To give life form.
A child's sand boat facing
the sun.
Plastic soldiers in the miniature
dirt war. Forts.
Garage Rocket Ships

Ceremonies, theatre, dances
To reassert
Tribal needs and memories
a call to worship, uniting
above all, a reversion,
a longing for family and the
safety magic of childhood

A man rakes leaves into
a heap in his yard, a pile,
and leans on his rake and
burns them utterly.

The fragrance fills the forest

children pause and heed the
smell, which will become
nostalgia in several years.

An angel runs
Thru the sudden light
Thru the room
A ghost precedes us
A shadow follows us
And each time we stop
We fall

The Endless quest a vigil
of watchtowers and fortresses
against the sea and time.
Have they won? Perhaps.
They still stand and in
their silent rooms still wander
the souls of the dead,
who keep their watch on the living.
Soon enough we shall join them.
Soon enough we shall walk
the walls of time. We shall
miss nothing
except each other.

No one thought up being;
he who thinks he has
Step forward

The Crossroads
a place where ghosts
reside to whisper into
the ears of travelers &

interest them in their fate

Hitchhiker drinks:
"I call again on the dark
hidden gods of blood"

—Why do you call us?
You know our price. It
never changes. Death of
you will give you life
& free you from a vile
fate. But it is getting late.

—If I could see you again
& talk w/ you, & walk a
short while in your company,
& drink the heady brew
of your conversations,
I thought

—to rescue a soul already
ruined. To achieve respite.
To plunder green gold
on a pirate raid & bring
to camp the glory of old.

—As the capesman faces
poisoned horns & drinks
red victory; the soldier,
too, w/ his trophy, a
pierced helmet; & the
ledge-walker shuddering
his way into inward grace

—(laughter) Well, then. Would

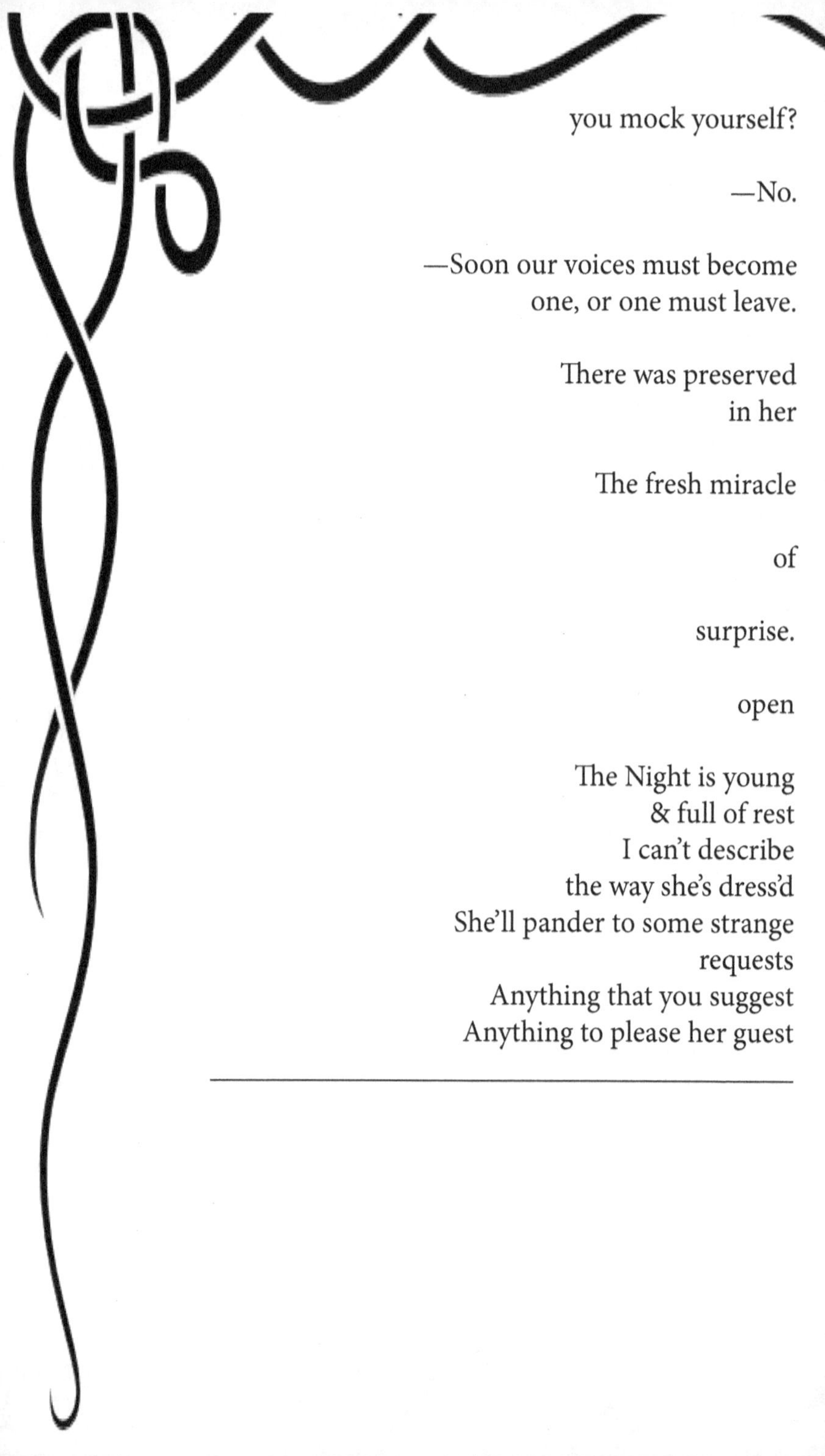

you mock yourself?

—No.

—Soon our voices must become
one, or one must leave.

There was preserved
in her

The fresh miracle

of

surprise.

open

The Night is young
& full of rest
I can't describe
the way she's dress'd
She'll pander to some strange
requests
Anything that you suggest
Anything to please her guest

AWAKE

Shake dreams from your hair
My pretty child, my sweet one.
Choose the day and
choose the sign of your day
The day's divinity
First thing you see.
A vast radiant beach
in a cool jeweled moon
Couples naked race down by it's quiet side
And we laugh like soft, mad children
Smug in the woolly cotton brains of infancy
The music and voices are all around us.
Choose, they croon, the Ancient Ones
The time has come again
Choose now, they croon,
Beneath the moon
Beside an ancient lake
Enter again the sweet forest
Enter the hot dream
Come with us
Everything is broken up and dances.

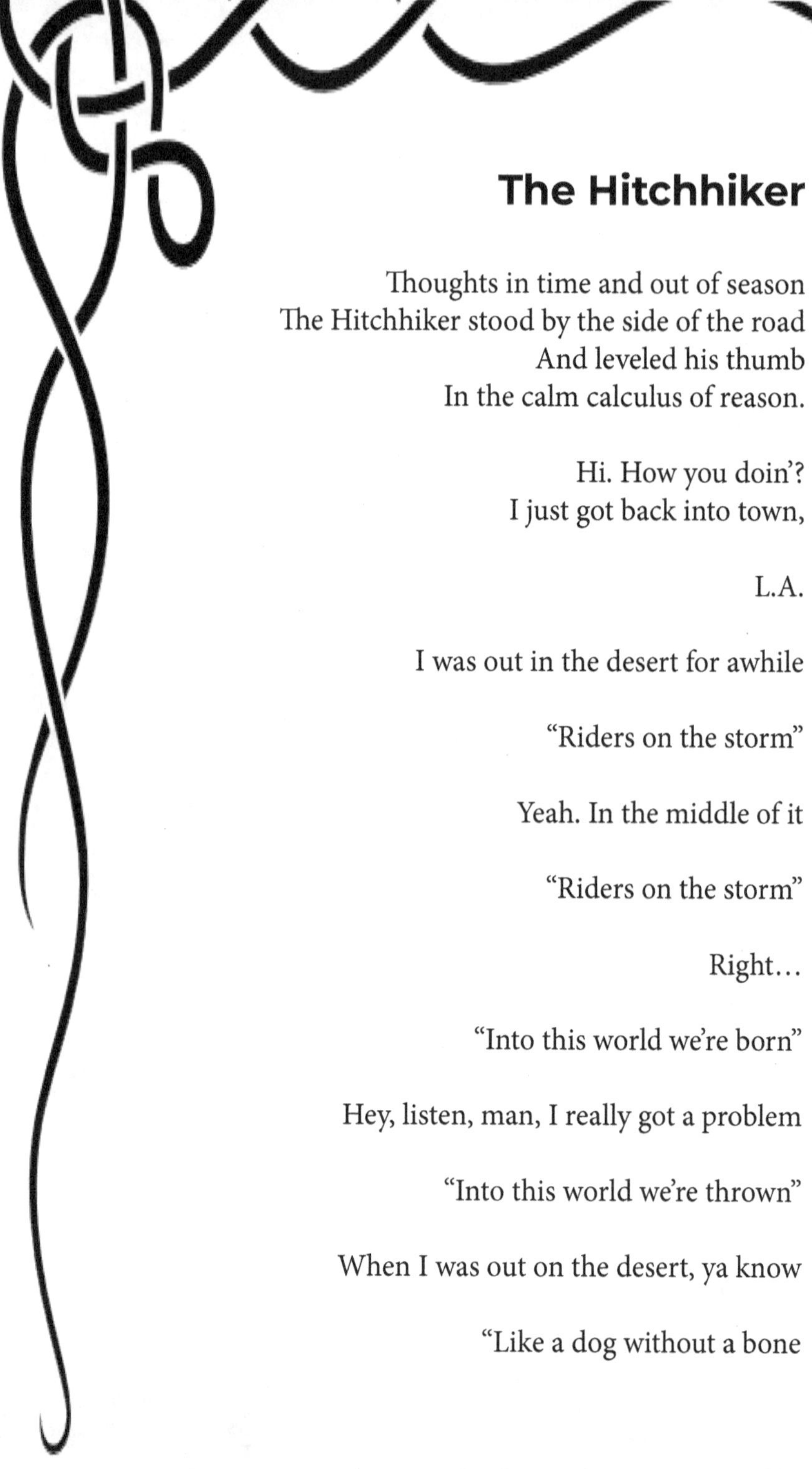

The Hitchhiker

Thoughts in time and out of season
The Hitchhiker stood by the side of the road
And leveled his thumb
In the calm calculus of reason.

Hi. How you doin'?
I just got back into town,

L.A.

I was out in the desert for awhile

"Riders on the storm"

Yeah. In the middle of it

"Riders on the storm"

Right…

"Into this world we're born"

Hey, listen, man, I really got a problem

"Into this world we're thrown"

When I was out on the desert, ya know

"Like a dog without a bone

An actor out on loan"

I don't know how to tell you

"Riders on the storm"

but, ah, I killed somebody

"There's a killer on the road"

No…

"His brain is squirming like a toad"

It's no big deal, ya know

I don't think anybody will find out about it, but…

"take a long holiday"

just, ah…

"Let your children play"

this guy gave me a ride, and ah…

"If you give this man a ride"

started giving me a lot of trouble

"Sweet family will die"

and I just couldn't take it, ya know

"Killer on the road"

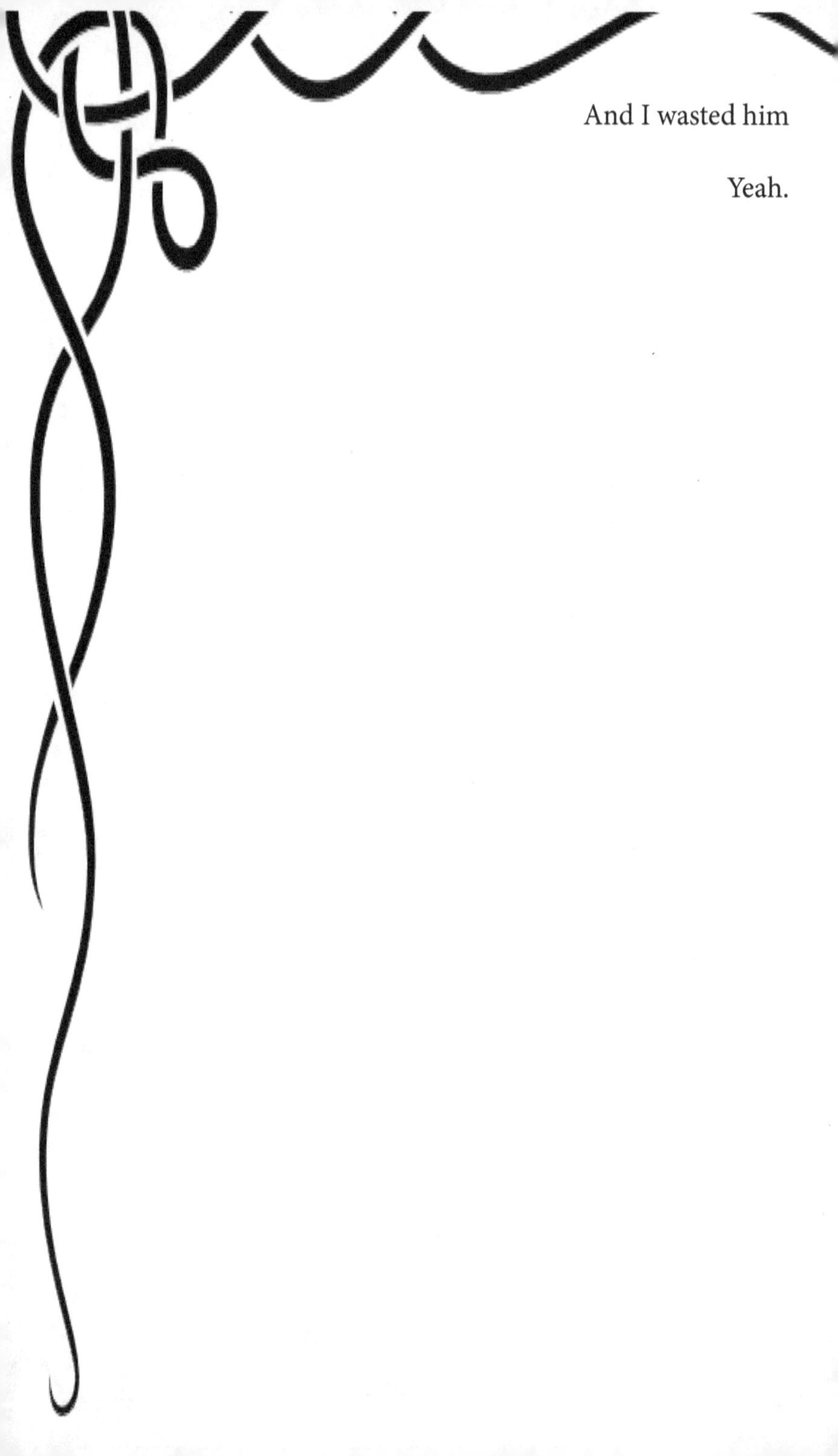

And I wasted him

Yeah.

The American Night

for leather accrues
The miracle of the streets
The scents & smogs &
pollens of existence

Shiny blackness
so totally naked she was
Totally un-hung-up

We looked around
lights now on
Top see our fellow travellers
~~~
I am troubled
Immeasurably
By your eyes

I am struck
By the feather
of your soft
Reply

The sound of glass
Speaks quick
Disdain

And conceals
What your eyes fight
To explain
~~~

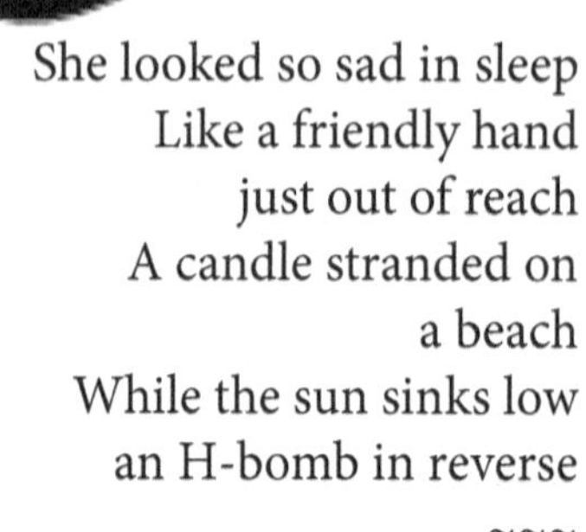

She looked so sad in sleep
Like a friendly hand
just out of reach
A candle stranded on
a beach
While the sun sinks low
an H-bomb in reverse

~~~

Everything human
is leaving
her face

Soon she will disappear
into the calm
vegetable
morass

Stay!

My Wild Love!

~~~

I get my best ideas when the
telephone rings & rings. It's no fun
To feel like a fool-when your
baby's gone. A new ax to my head:
Possession. I create my own sword
of Damascus. I've done nothing w/time.
A little tot prancing the boards playing
w/Revolution. When out there the
World awaits & abounds w/heavy gangs
of murderers & real madmen. Hanging
from windows as if to say: I'm bold-

do you love me? Just for tonight.
A One Night Stand. A dog howls & whines
at the glass sliding door (why can't I
be in there?) A cat yowls. A car engine
revs & races against the grain- dry
rasping carbon protest. I put the book
down- & begin my own book.
Love for the fat girl.
When will SHE get here?
~~~

In the gloom
In the shady living room
where we lived & died
& laughed & cried
& the pride of our relationship
took hold that summer
What a trip
To hold your hand
& tell the cops
you're not 16
no runaway
The wino left a little in
the old blue desert
bottle
Cattle skulls
the cliche of rats
who skim the trees
in search of fat
Hip children invade the grounds
& sleep in the wet grass
'til the dogs rush out
I'm going South!

Immaculate
~~~

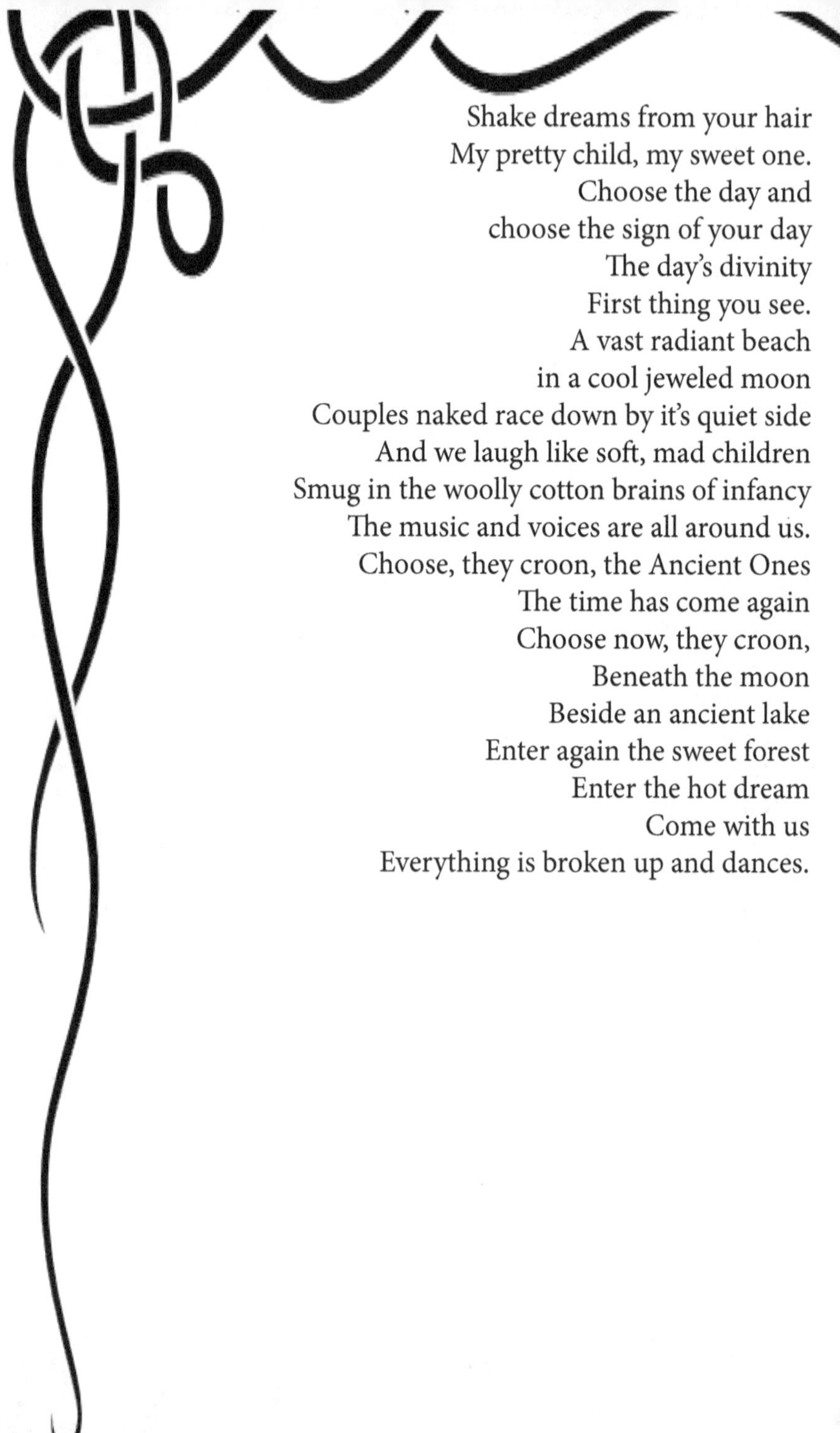

Shake dreams from your hair
My pretty child, my sweet one.
Choose the day and
choose the sign of your day
The day's divinity
First thing you see.
A vast radiant beach
in a cool jeweled moon
Couples naked race down by it's quiet side
And we laugh like soft, mad children
Smug in the woolly cotton brains of infancy
The music and voices are all around us.
Choose, they croon, the Ancient Ones
The time has come again
Choose now, they croon,
Beneath the moon
Beside an ancient lake
Enter again the sweet forest
Enter the hot dream
Come with us
Everything is broken up and dances.

Power

I can make the earth stop in
its tracks. I made the
blue cars go away.
I can make myself invisible or small.
I can become gigantic and reach the
farthest things. I can change
the course of nature.
I can place myself anywhere in
space or time.
I can summon the dead.
I can perceive events on other worlds,
in my deepest inner mind,
and in the minds of others.
I can.
I am.

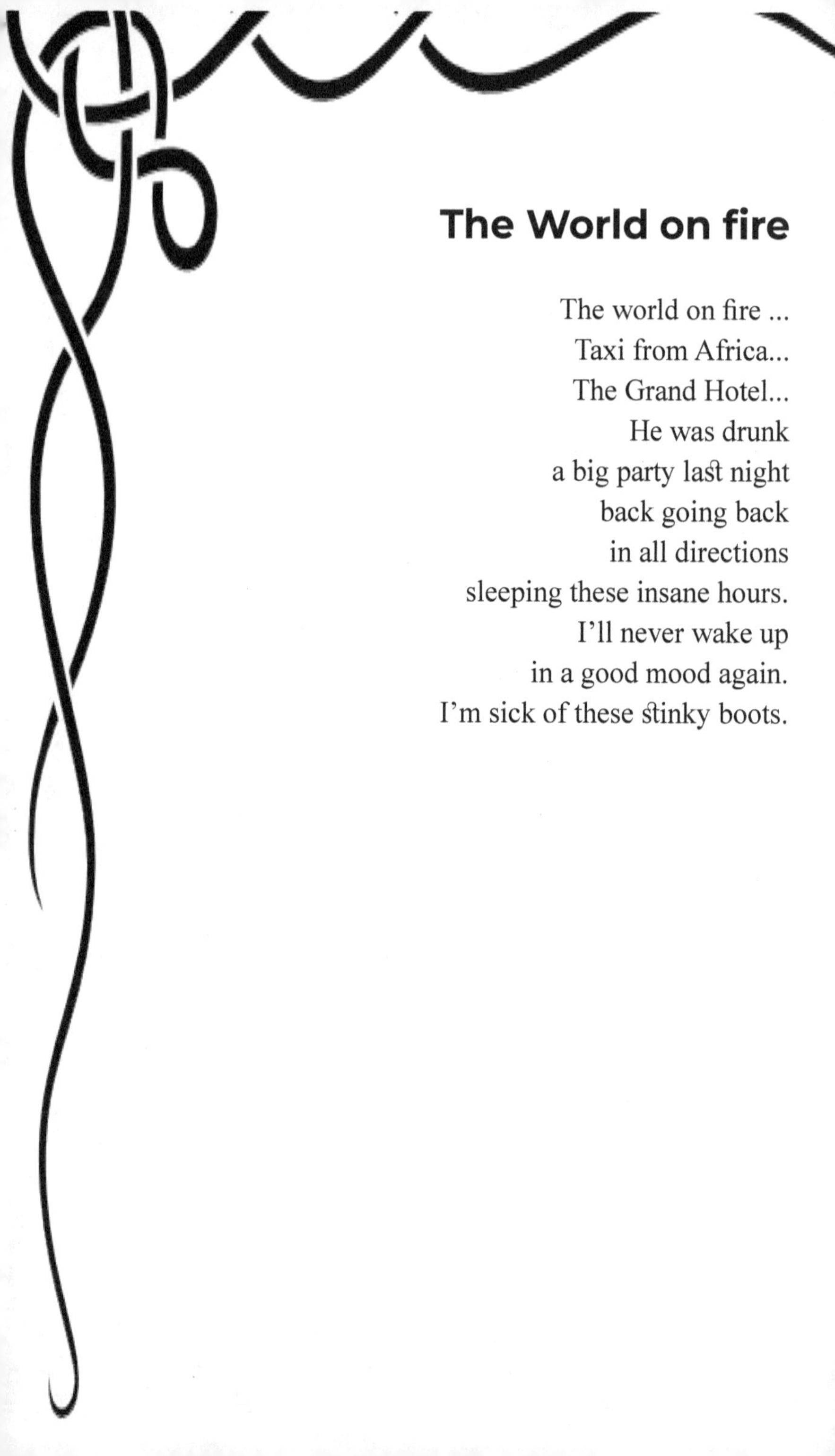

The World on fire

The world on fire ...
Taxi from Africa...
The Grand Hotel...
He was drunk
a big party last night
back going back
in all directions
sleeping these insane hours.
I'll never wake up
in a good mood again.
I'm sick of these stinky boots.

The Movie

The movie will begin in five moments.
The mindless voice announced
all those unseated will await the next show.
We filed slowly, languidly into the hall.

The auditorium was vast and silent
as we seated and were darkened, the voice continued.
The program for this evening is not new.
You've seen this entertainment through and through.
You've seen your birth your life and death
you might recall all of the rest.

Did you have a good world when you died?
Enough to base a movie on?
I'm getting out of here.
Where are you going?
To the other side of morning.

Please don't chase the clouds, pagodas.
Her cunt gripped him like a warm, friendly hand.
It's alright, all your friends are here.

When can I meet them?
After you've eaten
I'm not hungry.
Uh, we meant beaten.
Silver stream, silvery scream.
Oooooh, impossible concentration.

Newborn Awakening

Gently they stir, gently rise.
The dead are newborn awakening.
With ravaged limbs and wet souls.
Gently they sigh in rapt funeral amazement.
Who called these dead to dance?

Was it the young woman learning to play the ghost song on
her baby grand?
Was it the wilderness children?
Was it the ghost god himself, stuttering, cheering, chatting
blindly?

I called you up to anoint the earth.
I called you to announce sadness falling like burned skin.
I called you to wish you well.
To glory in self like a new monster.
And now I call you to pray.

Stoned Inmaculate

I'll tell you this...
No eternal reward will forgive us now.
For wasting the dawn.
Back in those days everything was simpler and more confused.

One summer night, going to the pier.
I ran into two young girls.
The blonde one was called Freedom.
The dark one, Enterprise.
We talked and they told me this story.
Now listen to this...

I'll tell you about Texas radio and the big beat.
Soft driven, slow and mad.
Like some new language.
Reaching your head with the cold, sudden fury of a divine messenger.
Let me tell you about heartache and the loss of god.
Wandering, wandering in hopeless night.

Out here in the perimeter there are no stars.
Out here we is stoned.
Immaculate.

Freedom Exists

Did you know freedom exists
In school books
Did you know madmen are
Running our prisons

Within a jail, within a gaol
Within a white free protestant
Maelstrom

We're perched headlong
On the edge of boredom
We're reaching for death
On the end of a candle
We're trying for something
That's already found us

Ghost Song

Awake.
Shake dreams from your hair
My pretty child, my sweet one.
Choose the day and choose the sign of your day
The days divinity
First thing you see.

A vast radiant beach in a cool jeweled moon
Couples naked race down by its quiet side
And we laugh like soft, mad children
Smug in the wooly cotton brains of infancy
The music and voices are all around us.

Choose they croon the ancient ones
The time has come again
Choose now, they croon
Beneath the moon
Beside an ancient lake
Enter again the sweet forest
Enter the hot dream
Come with us.

Everything is broken up and dance.
Indians scattered,
On dawn's highway bleeding
Ghosts crowd the young child's,
Fragile eggshell mind

We have assembled inside,

This ancient and insane theater
To propagate our lust for life,
And flee the swarming wisdom of the streets.

The barns have stormed
The windows kept,
And only one of all the rest
To dance and save us
From the divine mockery of words,
Music inflames temperament.

Ooh great creator of being
Grant us one more hour,
To perform our art
And perfect our lives.

We need great golden copulations,

When the true kings murderers
Are allowed to roam free,
A thousand magicians arise in the land
Where are the feast we are promised?

Hour For Magic

Resident mockery
give us an hour for magic
We of the purple glove
We of the starling flight
and velvet hour

We of Arabic pleasure's breed
We of sundome and the night
Give us a creed
To believe

A Night of lust
Give us trust in
The Night
Give of color
Hundred hues
a rich mandala
For me and you

And for your silky
pillowed house
A head, wisdom
And a bed
Troubled decree
Resident mockery
has claimed thee.

We used to believe.
In the good old days.
We still receive in

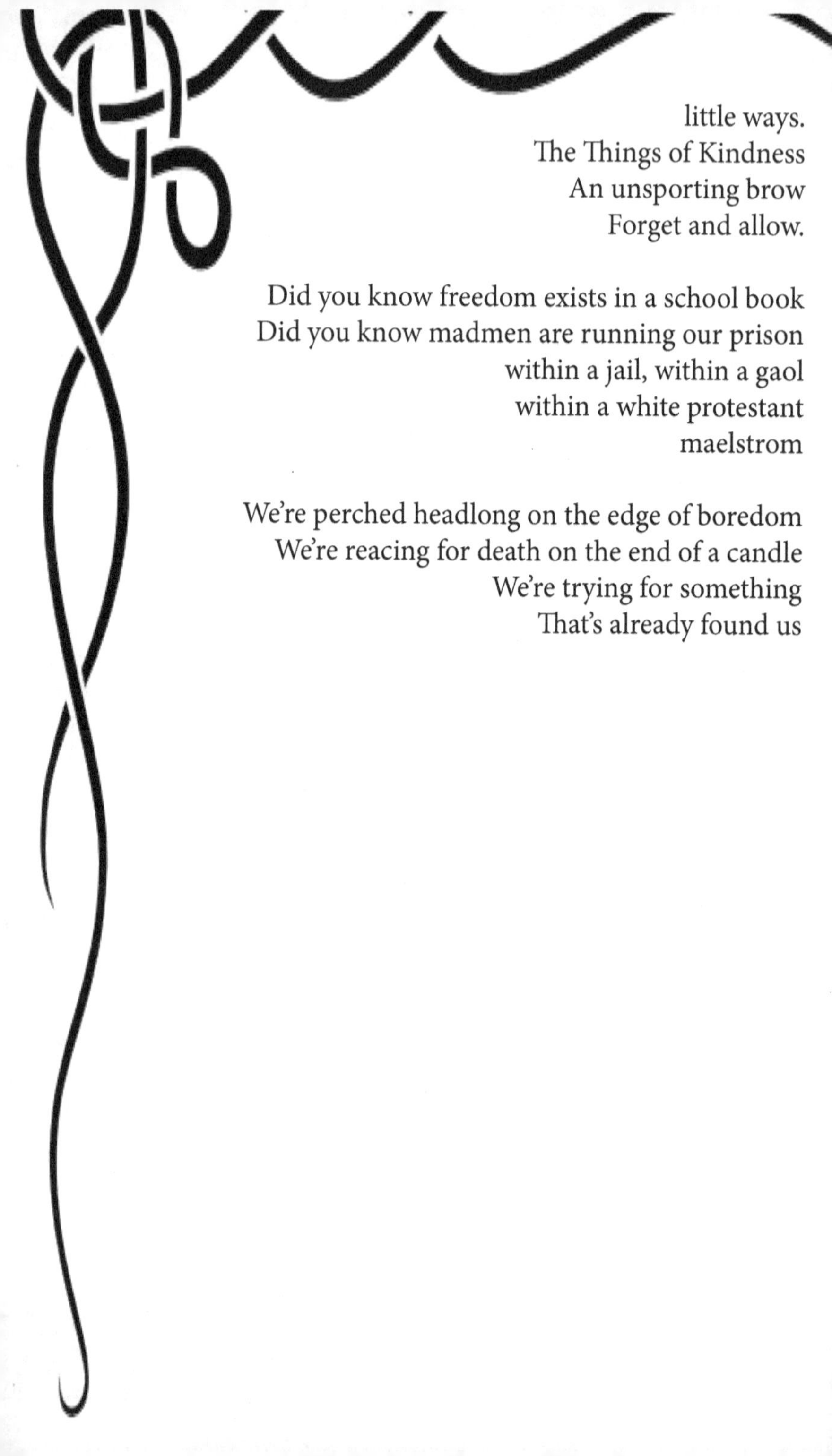

little ways.
The Things of Kindness
An unsporting brow
Forget and allow.

Did you know freedom exists in a school book
Did you know madmen are running our prison
within a jail, within a gaol
within a white protestant
maelstrom

We're perched headlong on the edge of boredom
We're reacing for death on the end of a candle
We're trying for something
That's already found us

Lament

Lament for my cock
Sore and crucified
I seek to know you
Acquiring soulful wisdom
You can open walls of mystery
Stripshow

How to acquire death in the morning show
TV death which the child absorbs
Deathwell mystery which makes me write
Slow train, the death of my cock gives life
Forgive the poor old people who gave us entry
Taught us god in the child's prayer in the night

Guitar player
Ancient wise satyr
Sing your ode to my cock
Caress it's lament
Stiffen and guide us, we frozen

Lost cells
The knowledge of cancer
To speak to the heart
And give the great gift
Words Power Trance
This stable friend and the beast of his zoo
Wild haired chicks
Women flowering in their summit

Monsters of skin

Each color connects
to create the boat
which rocks the race
Could any hell be more horrible
than now
and real?

I pressed her thigh and death smiled
Death, old friend
Death and my cock are the world
I can forgive my injuries in the name of
Wisdom Luxury Romance
Sentence upon sentence
Words are the healing lament
For the death of my cock's spirit
Has no meaning in the soft fire
Words got me the wound and will get me well
I you believe it

All join now and lament the death of my cock
A tounge of knowledge in the feathered night
Boys get crazy in the head and suffer
I sacrifice my cock on the altar of silence

A Feast of Friends

Wow, I'm sick of doubt
Live in the light of certain
South
Cruel bindings.

The servants have the power
dog-men and their mean women
pulling poor blankets over
our sailors
(And where were you in our lean hour)
Milking your moustache
or grinding a flower?

I'm sick of dour faces
Staring at me from the TV
Tower, I want roses in
my garden bower; dig?
Royal babies, rubies
must now replace aborted
Strangers in the mud
These mutants, blood-meal
for the plant that's plowed.

They are waiting to take us into
the severed garden
Do you know how pale and wanton thrillful
comes death on a strange hour
unannounced, unplanned for
like a scaring over-friendly guest you've
brought to bed

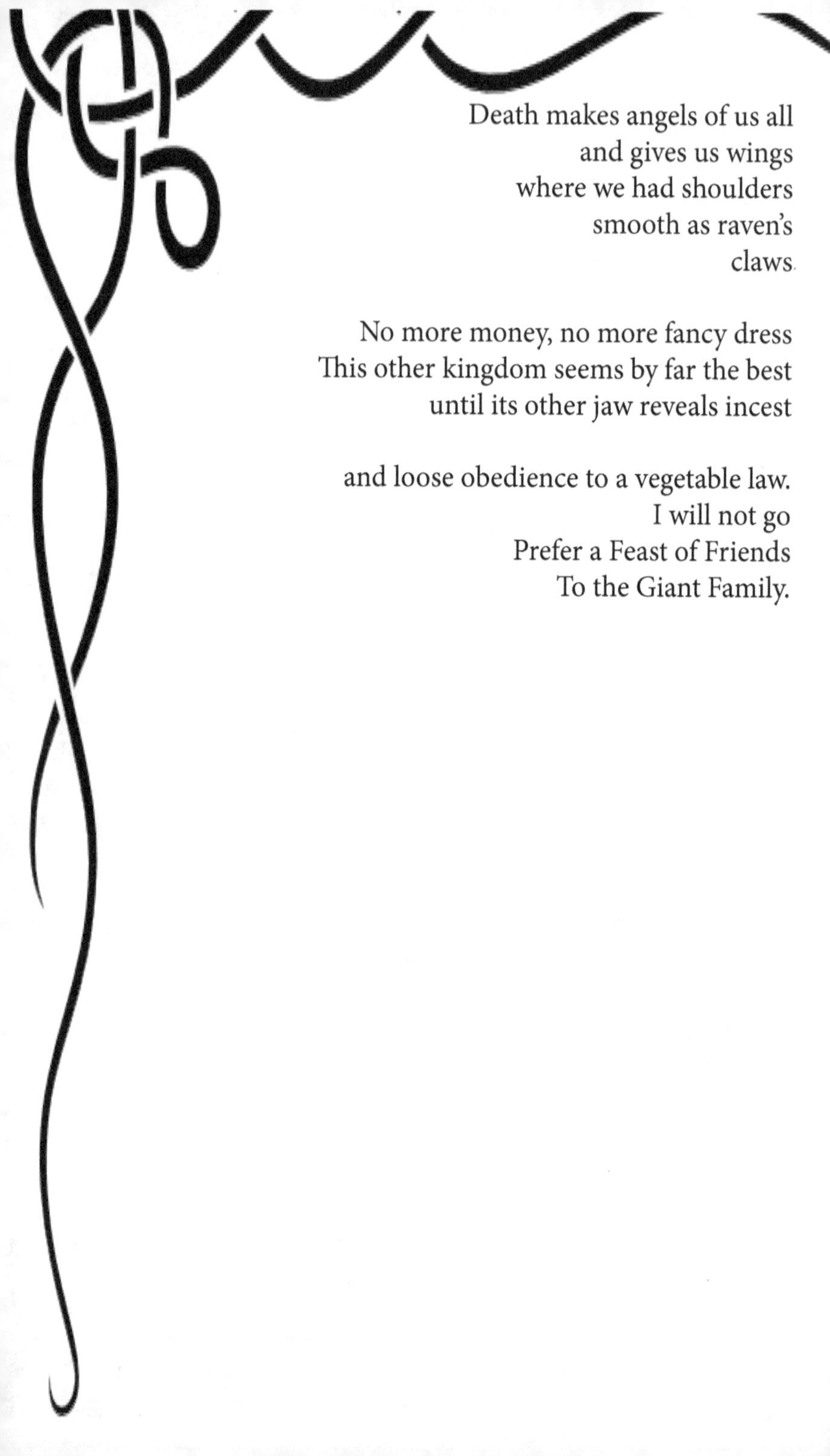

Death makes angels of us all
and gives us wings
where we had shoulders
smooth as raven's
claws.

No more money, no more fancy dress
This other kingdom seems by far the best
until its other jaw reveals incest

and loose obedience to a vegetable law.
I will not go
Prefer a Feast of Friends
To the Giant Family.

The Opening of the Trunk

Moment of inner freedom
when the mind is opened & the
infinite universe revealed
& the soul is left to wander
dazed & confus'd searching
here & there for teachers & friends.

Moment of Freedom
as the prisoner
blinks in the sun
like a mole
from his hole

a child's 1st trip
away from home

That moment of Freedom

LAmerica
Cold treatment of our empress
LAmerica
The Transient Universe
LAmerica
Instant communion and
communication
lamerica
emeralds in glass
lamerica
searchlights at twi-light
lamerica

streets in the pale dawn
lamerica
robed in exile
lamerica
swift beat of a proud heart
lamerica
eyes like twenty
lamerica
swift dream
lamerica
frozen heart
lamerica
soldiers doom
lamerica
clouds & struggles
lamerica
Nighthawk
doomed from the start
lamerica
"That's how I met her,
lamerica
lonely & frozen
lamerica
& sullen, yes
lamerica
right from the start"

Then stop.
Go. The wilderness between.
Go round the march.

he enters stage:

Blood boots. Killer storm.

Fool's gold. God in a heaven.
Where is she?
Have you seen her?
Has anyone seen this girl?
snap shot (projected)
She's my sister.
Ladies & gentlemen:
please attend carefully to these words & events
It's your last chance, our last hope.
In this womb or tomb, we're free of the
swarming streets.
The black fever which rages is safely
out those doors
My friends & I come from
Far Arden w/ dances, &
new music
Everywhere followers accrue
to our procession.
Tales of Kings, gods, warriors
and lovers dangled like
jewels for your careless pleasure

I'm Me!

Can you dig it.
My meat is real.
My hands- how they move
balanced like lithe demons
My hair- so twined & writhing
The skin of my face- pinch the cheeks
My flaming sword tongue
spraying verbal fire-flys
I'm real.
I'm human

But I'm not an ordinary man
No No No

What are you doing here?
What do you want?
Is it music?
We can play music.
But you want more.
You want something & someone new.
Am I right?
Of course I am.
I know what you want.
You want ecstasy
Desire & dreams.
Things not exactly what they seem.
I lead you this way, he pulls that way.
I'm not singing to an imaginary girl.
I'm talking to you, my self.
Let's recreate the world.
The palace of conception is burning.

Look. See it burn.
Bask in the warm hot coals.

You're too young to be old.
You don't need to be told
You want to see things as they are.
You know exactly what I do
Everything

I am a guide to the Labyrinth

Monarch of the protean towers
on this cool stone patio

above the iron mist
sunk in its own waste
breathing its own breath

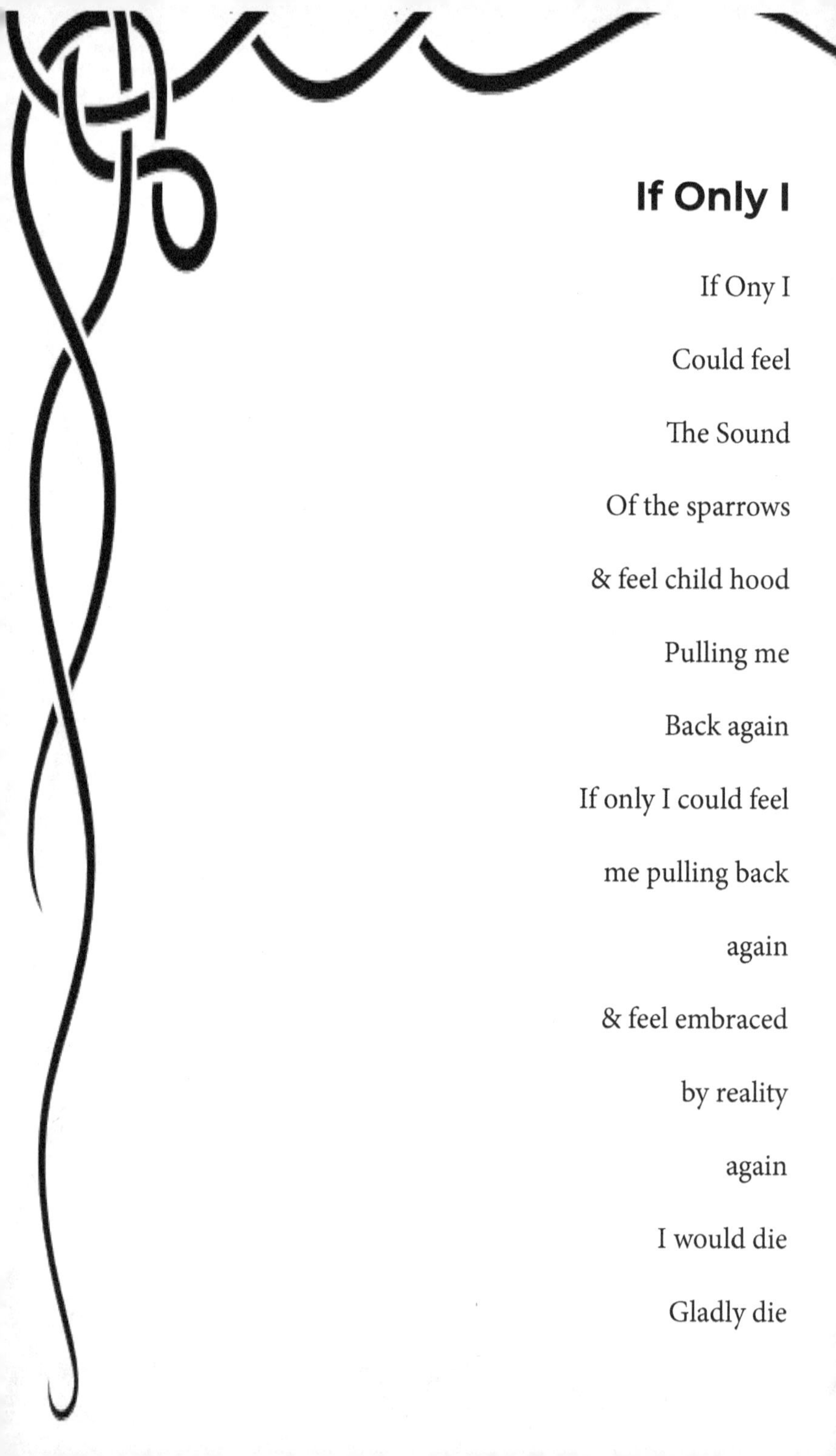

If Only I

If Ony I

Could feel

The Sound

Of the sparrows

& feel child hood

Pulling me

Back again

If only I could feel

me pulling back

again

& feel embraced

by reality

again

I would die

Gladly die

JIM MORRISON QUOTES

Some of the Worst Mistakes of my life have been Haircuts.

Blake said that the body was the soul's prison unless the five senses are fully developed and open. He considered the senses the 'windows of the soul.' When sex involves all the senses intensely, it can be like a mystical experience.

Film spectators are quiet vampires.

I am interested in anything about revolt, disorder, chaos-especially activity that seems to have no meaning. It seems to me to be the road toward freedom... Rather than starting inside, I start outside and reach the mental through the physical.

I think of myself as an intelligent, sensitive human being with the soul of a clown which always forces me to blow it at the most important moments.

I believe in a long, prolonged, derangement of the senses in order to obtain the unknown.

Friends can help each other. A true friend is someone who lets you have total freedom to be yourself - and especially to feel. Or, not feel. Whatever you happen to be feeling at the moment is fine with them. That's what real love amounts to - letting a person be what he really is.

People fear death even more than pain. It's strange that they fear death. Life hurts a lot more than death. At the point of death, the pain is over. Yeah, I guess it is a friend.

The appeal of cinema lies in the fear of death.

It's like gambling somehow. You go out for a night of

drinking and you don't know where you're going to end up the next day. It could work out good or it could be disastrous. It's like the throw of the dice.

Violence isn't always evil. What's evil is the infatuation with violence.

We fear violence less than our own feelings. Personal, private, solitary pain is more terrifying than what anyone else can inflict.

Drugs are a bet with your mind.

Whoever controls the media, controls the mind.

Listen, real poetry doesn't say anything; it just ticks off the possibilities. Opens all doors. You can walk through any one that suits you.

A Friend is someone who gives you total freedom to be yourself.

When you make your peace with Authority, You become Authority.

Music Inflames Temperament.

The most important kind of freedom is to be what you really are. You trade in your reality for a role. You give up your ability to feel, and in exchange, put on a mask.

Love cannot save you from your own fate.

I think in art, but especially in films, people are trying to confirm their own existences.

If my poetry aims to achieve anything, it's to deliver people from the limited ways in which they see and feel.

I see myself as an intelligent, sensitive human, with the soul of a clown which forces me to blow it at the most important moments.

Expose yourself to your deepest fear; after that, fear has no power, and the fear of freedom shrinks and vanishes. You are free.

I'm interested in anything about revolt, disorder, chaos, especially activity that appears to have no meaning. It seems to me to be the road toward freedom.

Death makes angels of us all and gives us wings where we had shoulders smooth as ravens claws.

Each generation wants new symbols, new people, new names. They want to divorce themselves from their predecessors.

There are things known and things unknown and in between are the doors.